THE POWER OF ANTI-SEMITISM

The march to the Holocaust 1919-1939

THE POWER OF ANTI-SEMITISM; THE MARCH TO THE HOLOCAUST 1919-1939

An exhibition by

The Museum of World War II Boston

KENNETH W. RENDELL and

SAMANTHA HEYWOOD

Foreword by LOUISE MIRRER

Boston · 2016

Published in conjunction with the exhibition
Anti-Semitism 1919-1939,
held at the New-York Historical Society
April 12-July 31, 2016

ISBN 978-0-692-65067-7

FOREWORD

ANTI-SEMITISM, though rooted in the Middle Ages, is among the most wrenching topics of twentieth century history. Most of us today associate the dogma and its corresponding policies with Adolf Hitler's rise to power in Germany, beginning in the early 1930's. But the extraordinary collection assembled by world-renowned collector Kenneth Rendell for The Museum of World War II, Boston reveals a different timeline. A copy of the public announcement of the Treaty of Versailles terms, owned and annotated by Hitler, gives evidence of virulent anti-Semitic sentiments and policies spanning the entire interwar period, with Hitler, in 1919, writing that the Treaty paved the way for a 'Jewish dictate,' and that the 'Jews must therefore leave Germany'. Other materials in the collection, including anti-Semitic books and signs warn that 'Jews are not allowed' in restaurants or on park benches, and original anti-Semitic newspaper articles and cartoons similarly give evidence of a slow but steady indoctrination of citizens, both non-Jewish and Jewish in Germany long before Hitler came to power.

This new – and path-breaking – understanding of the trajectory of anti-Semitism in Europe is without a doubt of tremendous historical significance. Still, many have asked why an institution such as the New-York Historical Society, which focuses on New York and American history would organize an exhibition on the topic. For me, there are several simple, but significant, answers. First, the materials in The Museum of World War II collection illustrate the ease with which propaganda can sink its roots in any society, and the dangers of underestimating its power. Second, the moral questions raised by the rise of the Nazis in Germany transcend geographical boundaries, falling squarely on the permanent agenda of institutions such as ours that look to the lessons of history as a way of provoking contemporary audiences to reflect on the roles and responsibilities of individuals, organizations, and nations when confronted with injustice. Third, there is indeed a direct connection between anti-Semitism in Europe and the history of our city and nation. Who could gainsay the enormous impact of those who fled Europe in the wake of Nazism on our cultural institutions, our colleges and universities, our scientific institutions and organizations? A whole 'University in Exile' was founded in New York with some of Europe's most notable scholars as faculty; European artists and musicians formed the bedrock of our city's modern art museums, institutes, conservatories and concert halls in the 1930's and 40's; European scientists reshaped our universities' research programs.

Finally, the astonishing discoveries of The Museum of World War II collection underscore the old adage about the importance of history: how it is impossible to understand who we are today without knowing from where we came. With more than 200,000 New York City public school students learning history each year at the New-York Historical Society, this collection offers an incomparable opportunity to convey to young people why a significant part of our city's demographic came to be in New York; how this demographic, like so many immigrant groups today, sought not only economic opportunity but the much more basic right to live without fear or threat of violence because of their ethnicity or religious belief.

I am enormously grateful to Kenneth Rendell and The Museum of World War II, Boston, for their generosity in sharing this collection with us. I thank our Chairman Emeritus, Roger Hertog, for drawing the collection to my attention. As always, the enlightened support of New-York Historical's Board of Trustees, led by Chair Pam Schafler and Vice Chair Richard Reiss, is at the core of our work on this exhibition; it is our trustees' generosity and hard-work that make it possible for our institution to Make History Matter for the broadest possible public. Gifts from the Blavatnik Family Foundation, the Charina Endowment Fund, the Barbara K. and Ira A. Lipman Family, Ed and Sandy Meyer, Ann and Andrew Tisch, Lori and Mark Fife, Cheryl and Glen Lewy, Pam and Scott Schafler, the David Berg Foundation, Carol and Roger Einiger, Martin and Ahuva Gross, Ruth and Sid Lapidus, Martin Lewis and Diane Brandt, Sue Ann Weinberg, and Tamar J. Weiss have helped bring this exhibition to fruition. I recognize with gratitude their generous support.

Louise Mirrer, Ph.D.
President and CEO
New-York Historical Society

INTRODUCTION

T<small>HE CONCEPT</small> of this exhibition, 'The power of anti-Semitism 1919-1939, the march to the Holocaust', developed while expanding the number of antisemitic pieces on display at The Museum of World War II, Boston where we seek to better illustrate the incremental stages from 1919 to 1939 that led to the Holocaust. The Holocaust didn't just happen; anti-Semitism was gradually and systematically nurtured to make Germans accustomed to its rise, and readily acquiesce in new regulations limiting Jews and Jewish life. Each step was incremental, but the increments forcefully accumulated and led to the Holocaust.

The idea to bring the exhibition to New York was Roger Hertog's. He is one of the most critical and deep thinkers about important issues, and a person who acts on his beliefs. A conversation in his office about my observations on anti-Semitism quickly led to a phone call to President and CEO Louise Mirrer, and to this exhibition at the New-York Historical Society.

At The Museum of World War II Boston, our mission is to preserve the reality of World War II, its causes and consequences, and through the exhibits of original documents and artifacts, to illustrate the human stories in the political, social and military contexts. Our permanent exhibit on The Rise of Nazism begins with the earliest known handwritten antisemitic rant by Hitler (the first piece in this exhibit). Our permanent exhibit on the Holocaust begins with the original manuscript of Hitler's January 30, 1939 speech in the Reichstag in which he announces the 'annihilation' of the Jews (the final piece in this exhibition). In those twenty years, anti-Semitism was purposefully grown: first through Jewish exclusion from early Nazi Party rallies to gradual exclusion from every facet of life and then life itself. Anti-Semitism was orchestrated to both express the hatred of Nazi fanatics and to insidiously become part of the German way of life; to be accepted by the majority who would not on their own actually take action, and to exploit their fundamental resentment towards the Jews who were successful in German society disproportionate to their numbers.

While the Museum displays in-depth collections in every area and aspect of World War II, and vividly illustrates the causes and events of World War II, our exhibits on The Rise of Nazism and the Holocaust have the greatest impact, especially with students. Visitors personally experience the artifacts, as many can be touched and handled.

This intimacy is matched by a challenge to think critically: original source materials and not interpretative signage are used to convey the information that people at the time read. This philosophy especially bears fruit when visitors see the complexity of The Rise of Nazism: nationalism, pageantry, economics, revenge; but anti-Semitism is at the heart of the Nazi propaganda in all areas.

Anti-Semitism has a long and terrible history which is out of the purview of this exhibition. To put it into context: many legal barriers in Germany had been removed by the start of the twentieth century, though social barriers remained. Many young Jews were entering German universities and giving up traditional Jewish life. They were marrying non-Jews, converting to Christianity and becoming important in cultural, intellectual and business life. Jewish scientists, artists and writers were thriving and becoming leaders in German life. They served in the Great War, World War I, where over 12,000 died. They believed they were good Germans.

Adolf Hitler wrote in 'Mein Kampf', in 1925, about the origins of his own anti-Semitism. He states that he was not antisemitic before moving to Vienna and that the vilification of the German Kaiser in the mainstream press gradually led him to an antisemitic newspaper and then to antisemitic pamphlets. He began to see Jews not as 'Germans of a special religion, but a people in themselves' ('Mein Kampf'). He then began to see Jews as linked to what he saw as the greatest evil: Social Democracy and Marxism, and the lesser evils of unionism and the liberal press.

However, in his highly respected biography of Hitler, Ian Kershaw writes that Hitler is not necessarily to be believed, that 'Mein Kampf' was written for propaganda reasons. Kershaw's research led to the conclusion that it is impossible to determine with certainty why or when Hitler developed his particular brand of anti-Semitism. Initially in Vienna he apparently had Jewish friends in the Men's Home where he took refuge from his economically failed life. He apparently insisted that his paintings be sold thru Jewish dealers who he thought were better businessmen. Most probably, Hitler's anti-Semitism originated as a rationalization for his failure as an artist or architect. As Kershaw notes, anti-Semitism provided an explanation for Hitler's 'personal circumstances rather than a thought-out 'world-view'. It was a personalized hatred – blaming the Jews for all the ills that befell him in a city that he associated with personal misery. But any expression of this hatred that he had internalized did not stand out to those around him where antisemitic vitriol was so normal'.

Whatever its roots, by the end of World War I Hitler was verbally expressing rabid antisemitic views. With the signing of the Versailles Treaty, as seen in the first document in this exhibition, Hitler had convinced himself that the Jews were behind Germany's humiliation and the crippling reparations.

Hitler tapped into existing German prejudices against the Jew. His manic and obsessive anti-Semitism was personal, and while using it to bring crowds to a frenzy with his oratorical skills, he was also very clever in introducing it in propaganda very incrementally so that the majority of Germans who were not rabidly antisemitic acquiesced and accepted each level. German citizens were focused on inflation, unemployment, having lost the war and, through the hated Versailles Treaty, had been compelled to accept humiliating blame for the war, and pay reparations in gold. Hitler could appeal to them by blaming the Jews for all these problems but he had to cultivate his extreme views carefully, and he did.

When Hitler was released from Landsberg Prison in 1924 after his conviction for the Beer Hall Putsch in 1923, he was forbidden to make public speeches until 1927. He used this time to reorganize the Nazi Party and to moderate his anti-Semitism in areas of Germany where his strident attacks were not as yet accepted. Nuremburg, notably, was a strong point of anti-Jewish fervor. Julius Streicher, the regional leader, was one of the most virulent antisemites from 1923 to the end of the war. He created the newspaper *Der Stürmer* with violently racist caricatures and three children's books in later years (all are seen in this exhibition).

By the late 1920's, Hitler realized that the path to power was in democratic elections. His attacks on Jews almost disappeared. But in 1933, as soon as he was appointed Chancellor as the head of the largest elected party in Germany, he moved with breathtaking speed to ruthlessly eliminate all opposition and to force Jews to emigrate, having left behind nearly everything they possessed. (Their household goods were distributed to Aryan Germans thereby giving them a stake in Jews being forced to leave or sent to camps). As he annexed Austria in 1938, and anticipated attacking and conquering Poland in late 1939, he arrived at annihilation which he announced on the sixth anniversary of becoming Chancellor, January 30, 1939, in the Reichstag. The original manuscript of this speech is the last document in this exhibition.

With its state-sanctioned hatred, its increasingly restrictive and deadly laws, and its propaganda, German anti-Semitism was very different than that in the nations that became the Allies. Hitler describes in 'Mein Kampf' the great importance he placed on propaganda. Central to selling his antisemitic mission to the German people, this propaganda was focused on triggering emotions amongst large groups. Lies, exaggerated and endlessly repeated, are more effective than small lies, and crowds are easier to sway than individuals.

The events of 1919 to 1945 are deeply relevant today to understanding our world and the future, but, tragically, understanding the rise of anti-Semitism is critical in view of the current events in the world. This exhibition shows that good people today cannot accept any level of anti-Semitism or racial hatred as a fringe viewpoint to be tolerated. An understanding of the causes and consequences of World War II has led me to conclude that there are many people in the world to whom evil is a pleasure, an end in itself. Whether one believes that the Germans of the 1920's-1940's were a particularly compulsively orderly and obedient people who followed their evil leaders, or that inherent evilness only needed a cause to follow, it is important to appreciate the dangers in accepting anti-Semitism and racism on any level. As Otto Frank, Anne Frank's father, wrote, 'To build a future, you have to know the past'. Today, we have to know the past to understand the perils of today.

Kenneth W. Rendell
Founder and Executive Director
The Museum of World War II Boston

Catalogue

Münchner Neueste Nachrichten

München, 28. Juni 1919.

Die Unterzeichnung
des Friedensvertrages

WTB. **Versailles**, 28. Juni.

Der Friedensvertrag ist, wie vorgeschrieben, nachmittags 3 Uhr im Schlosse unterzeichnet worden.

Druck von Knorr & Hirth in München.

'The peace treaty aims at preparing Germany for the Jewish dictate...'

Hitler's earliest known handwritten antisemitic rant; broadsheet announcement of the terms of the Versailles Treaty, Münchner Neueste Nachrichten, 28 June 1919

This broadside announcing the signing of the peace treaty at Versailles was discovered in Hitler's papers from his Munich apartment. His handwritten comments may be his earliest known recorded antisemitic statement; *The peace treaty aims at preparing Germany for the Jewish dictate, the Versailles peace treaty makes the objective of Judah – the destruction of Germany – possible. The Jews must therefore leave Germany.*

The fact of Germany's defeat came as an enormous shock to most Germans, as the dramatic reversals of the war on the western front from August 1918 onwards had been deliberately concealed from them. By the end of September, the German army had retreated 25 miles along a 40 mile long front. Between August and November 1918 more German soldiers had been taken prisoner by Allied forces than during the whole of the rest of the war. The leaders of the Reichstag parties were not informed of this desperate situation until 2 October when the High Command recommended that Germany sue for peace. The German and Austrian people had already suffered through two years of serious hardship, hunger and in some areas, starvation, as a result of the British naval blockade. Social and industrial unrest was common. But by early November, the actions of mutinying sailors, workers and Communists had resulted in several large cities, including Berlin, being taken under the control of new, revolutionary soldiers' and workers' councils. In Munich a socialist uprising secured the abdication of the King of Bavaria on 7 November, bringing a 700-year dynasty to an abrupt end. Suddenly, the stability and strength of the entire German Empire seemed seriously undermined. The events in Russia, where the Bolshevik revolution of the year before had led to the violent termination of the Romanov era and dynasty and had plunged the country into devastating civil war, were very much present in the minds of the German High Command as they considered their options. By 9 November, Kaiser Wilhelm had abdicated, the Empire dissolved, and a new republic declared. Under these unprecedented and confused circumstances, it took a mere four days for terms of an armistice to be agreed.

For Corporal Adolf Hitler, 1918 was a year of extreme contrasts. In July he was awarded the Iron Cross First Class for 'personal bravery and general merit', a decoration rarely awarded to someone of his rank. His regiment had taken part in all phases of Germany's successful spring offensive on the western front. Germany's army had been victorious against the Russians in 1917, ending the war on the eastern front. It must have seemed that nothing could prevent a similar victory in western Europe. When news of the Kaiser's abdication and the armistice of 11 November reached Hitler, he was in hospital, recovering from a British gas attack in October that had temporarily blinded him. Like many other Germans, he found the news shocking, incredible and repugnant.

By the time the signing of the peace treaty was announced in June 1919, Hitler was still in the army and living in Munich. He had witnessed the declaration and bloody defeat of the Bavarian Soviet Republic in the city earlier that spring, and was part of a soldiers' committee investigating whether any members of his regiment had given support to the Communists. His comments written on this newspaper announcement reveal his obsessive conviction that Germany's utter defeat and capitulation could only be explained as being the result of a conspiracy. And his virulent anti-Semitism meant he lay blame for this conspiracy on 'the Jews'.

1920·1929

After Germany's defeat in World War I the state faced serious unrest and the threat of disintegration. Following the abdication of the Kaiser, the new Weimar government struggled to establish control or stability. Its unpopularity had been guaranteed when it signed the Versailles treaty which committed Germany to accepting responsibility for starting the war, and for making financial reparations to the countries it had fought. A series of assassinations and serious uprisings of both Communist and right-wing groups, including the Freikrops, blighted the earliest years of the Weimar Republic.

In 1920 the German Worker's Party in Munich (Hitler had joined the year before) renamed itself as the National Socialist German Worker's Party. It published its party program which was written by Hitler and Anton Drexler, founder of the party, in February. Hitler discovered his oratorical skills and his ability to intuit the issues that his audiences would respond to during these years. Despite this growth in popularity and support, their first attempt at taking power, in the so-called 'Beer Hall Putsch' in Munich in 1923, resulted only in Hitler's imprisonment. Banned from public speaking, he nevertheless determined that electoral politics would be a more successful way to achieve power. Hitler wrote his political thesis, 'Mein Kampf', whilst in prison. It was published in 1925 but few people paid notice.

Throughout the decade, Hitler and the Nazi party seized upon German political and economic unrest through mass rallies and increasingly virulent language that blamed the Jews for Germany's problems. What was at first small type at the bottom of broadsides indicating that Jews were not welcomed at these meetings became, by the end of the decade, more overt in publications such as Joseph Goebbels's malignant antisemitic attack in 'Das Buch Isidor' published in 1928. While Jews continued to flourish both culturally and economically many still did not believe that Hitler posed a real threat. But, the man whom many had dismissed as a fringe crank in the early 1920s was to become a sinister and powerful dictator just a few years later.

First political program of the National Socialist German Workers' Party (NSDAP), Anton Drexler (1884-1942) and Adolf Hitler (1889-1945), Munich, 24 February 1920

Hitler had joined one of the many small right wing political groups in Munich, the German Workers' Party, in September 1919. Germany was a country in considerable turmoil and there were many such groups forming, disbanding, forging or breaking alliances, and fighting each other on the streets. The city of Munich was a center of political activity where meetings at its beer halls drew large crowds of people some of whom were attracted by the prospect of violence. By February 1920, Hitler had drawn up this party program together with the original founder of the party, Anton Drexler. It was introduced at a meeting at the Hofbräuhaus on 24 February to which nearly 2,000 people turned up. Hitler was not the main speaker, but when he spoke, some of the crowd became vociferous and violence broke out. However, he managed to overcome the noise and confusion to speak in its favor, and the program was adopted.

This document clearly identifies three fundamental principles that were to underpin Nazi ideology and policy for the next twenty-five years;

> 'We demand equality of rights for the German people in respect to the other nations; abrogation of the peace treaties of Versailles and St Germain [between the Allies and Austria].
>
> We demand land and territory (colonies) for the sustenance of our people, and colonization for our surplus population.
>
> Only a member of the race can be a citizen. A member of the race can only be one who is of German blood, without consideration of creed. Consequently no Jew can be a member of the race.'

Thirty-two nations had been involved in the peace talks in Paris in 1919, but representatives of the German government were not invited to attend until it was time for them to receive the peace terms that the Allied nations had agreed on. They were given three weeks to comply, with the understanding that if they did not, war would re-commence. 1919 had been a year filled with revolutionary violence and instability in Germany and in other countries too. The Spartacist Uprising in Berlin, and the Bavarian Soviet Republic had both been suppressed by the summer, but fears of further unrest were still high. The Social Democratic government accepted the terms under protest. Germany was stripped of all its overseas colonies, nearly half of its iron industry, a quarter of its coal industry, 12% of its population and 10% of its European territory. It was forced to accept the clause stating that Germany was guilty of starting the war, to undertake to pay reparations and to severely limit the size of its armed forces.

These terms are not as severe as those Germany had imposed on Russia in 1917 by the Treaty of Brest-Litovsk. But Hitler was not alone in his view that Versailles had been an utter betrayal of the German people by politicians – a 'stab in the back'– and that the terms were far too punitive. Along with many other right wing and antisemitic Germans, he laid the blame on

Jews. Such a betrayal was inexplicable, in Hitler's mind, without there being a substantial and deliberate conspiracy to destroy Germany. What is particularly interesting is the emphasis that this program of 1920 places on the other two principles – demands for land, which would later be referred to as 'Lebensraum', and for German citizenship to be based on a definition of race which excluded Jews, and that Jews would, therefore, have to leave Germany.

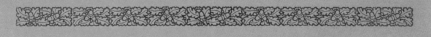

✒ National Socialist German Workers' Party (NSDAP) broadside, 3 February 1921

This poster was produced to publicize the largest meeting yet organized by the National Socialist German Workers' Party (NSDAP, but more commonly referred to as 'Nazi'), on 3 February 1921. The inflammatory wording for it was dictated by Hitler, protesting against the payment of reparations by Germany as required by the Versailles settlement; *Whoever wants to live should come and protest against the fact that we are being robbed of our ability to live'*. Typically, this poster advises that Jews will not be granted entry to the meeting.

The Nazi Party was one of many, tiny but vociferous, political groups in Germany at this time. Hitler was elected its leader in July 1921. His first attempt at seizing power on a larger scale – the Munich 'Beer Hall Putsch' (8/9 November 1923) had been a complete failure. He was imprisoned and the Nazi Party banned. Activity continued in alliance with other like-minded groups, as this poster announcing a meeting of The Völkische Block shows. Hitler was released from prison in December 1924, having written his political work, 'Mein Kampf' and resolved that the way to national power was to exploit electoral politics.

Promotional postcard for the Bahnhof Hotel Kölnerhof,
c. 1909, Frankfurt am Main

This postcard depicts the dining room of the Bahnhof Hotel Kölnerhof, Frankfurt am Main. It is an unremarkable image except for the sign affixed to the central column of the room which reads 'Judischer Besuch Verbeten' [sic] ('Jewish visitors prohibited'). It is probable that this postcard dates from before the First World War. The Hotel Kölnerhof was owned by Hermann Laass who, from 1895 onwards, openly advertised it as a 'Jew-free' hotel. He produced a range of postcards, stamps and stickers to promote this marketing message until the outbreak of the First World War in 1914. Advertisements for the hotel published in newspapers contained the same messaging. The postcard is an interesting insight into the kind of anti-Semitism that existed prior to that of Nazism, advocating a shameless exclusion of Jews from everyday social life.

Anti-Semitism had been an increasing phenomenon in Germany since the economic crash and depression of the 1870s and gained support throughout that decade and into the late 1880s, as conservative nationalist groups and parties also grew in strength. But anti-Semitism considerably predates this. Hatred of Jews is perhaps 'the longest hatred', dating back to the first millennium of the Christian era, when Jews were held responsible for the death of Christ. Following the destruction of the Temple by the Romans, Jews were ejected from their lands. Theological differences, and the fact that Jews were now a diaspora and outsiders, meant that fears and myths proliferated. One of the most persistent myths was that Jews used the blood of Christian children in their rituals. Another held that their refusal to convert to Christianity was a sign that they were in fact worshippers of the anti-Christ – the devil. Their separateness of faith and often, of their social and economic lives, only served to heighten the feelings of fear, distrust and alienation that the majority Christian populations of medieval Europe developed about Jewish people and communities. Natural and economic disasters were often blamed on the Jews and violence – pogroms – broke out at such times, where Jewish people and property were attacked.

During the early modern period of European history, the position of Jews began to change, as commerce, finance, manufacturing and free professions developed. Some rulers of this period allowed Jews to settle in their territories, and often, to take up work that the ruling classes did not wish to do themselves – moneylending, banking and other commercial activity. But Jews were also still at risk of wholescale persecution and expulsion from their homes and livelihoods during times of political, religious or economic turmoil. They were easily identifiable scapegoats. With the Enlightenment and the notion of equality under the law, many European states lifted legal restrictions on residence and occupations for Jews.

The vast majority of the Jewish population lived in eastern Europe on lands governed by the Russian Empire. The most widely published antisemitic text of modern times also originated from Russia in 1903. 'The Protocols of the Elders of Zion' purported to be a record of secret meetings of Jewish leaders that revealed a conspiracy to dominate the world. In fact, it was written under the direction of the Russian secret police and was exposed as a fraud as early as 1920, the same year that Henry Ford published a version of it for American readers. But it remains hugely influential to those seeking evidence for their antisemitic beliefs. For antisemites in early twentieth century Europe it served to confirm one of the other most powerful myths about Jews – that they were joined in a conspiracy to dominate the world for their own benefit and to the detriment of all non-Jews.

'Die Juden in der Karikatur' by Edward Fuchs (1870-1940),
published 1921, Munich

This book was one of a series of well-researched books on caricatures which covered other subjects such as women, erotic art, and the First World War. This volume contains reproductions of both well known and rare caricatures of Jews from the thirteenth century onwards and from a variety of countries including Germany, Austria, America, Britain, Russia and France. They depict the range of stereotypes from Jews as moneylenders, Bolsheviks, and sexual predators. Interestingly, the foreword's author, Edward Fuchs, was a Marxist, who left Germany when the Nazis came to power in 1933.

'A contemporary snapshot full of laughter and hate.'

Das Buch Isidor. Ein Zeitbild voll Lachen und Hass, Joseph Goebbels (1897-1945)
and Mjölnir, published 1928, Munich

'Das Buch Isidor', published in 1928, was part of Joseph Goebbels's campaign against Bernhard
Weiß, the Jewish Vice President of Berlin's police force. It includes many cartoons from the
Nazi newspaper 'Der Angriff' ('The Attack') that Goebbels established in 1927 whilst banned
from public speaking in Bavaria. 'Isidor' is a contemptuous name used to refer to Jews, whilst
'Mjölnir' refers to Thor's hammer, a brutally efficient and effective fighting tool. The book's
subtitle translates as; 'a contemporary snapshot full of laughter and hate'. Weiß repeatedly and
successfully sued Goebbels for defamation, but could not silence him and left Germany in 1933.

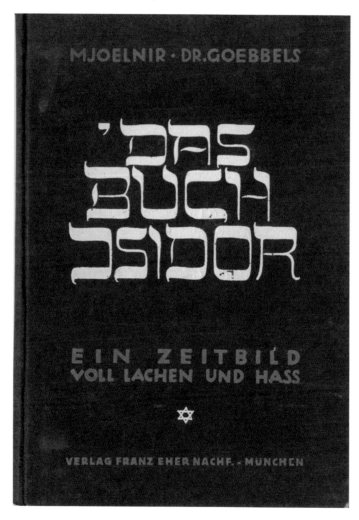

Postcard, *'Einst und Jetzt'*, undated

This undated postcard illustrates one of the most fundamental anxieties and prejudices about Jews, namely that they were growing fat through their plunder and exploitation of German society and resources. Even if they entered the country as poor immigrants – as depicted by the figure on the left of the postcard with the word 'Einst' ('then') – they would all too quickly become rich. This image of parasitism, of the enriched Jew making no active contribution to the economic vitality of the country, is reinforced by the depiction of the reclining, fat Jew, languorously smoking beneath the satisfied word 'Jetzt' ('Now').

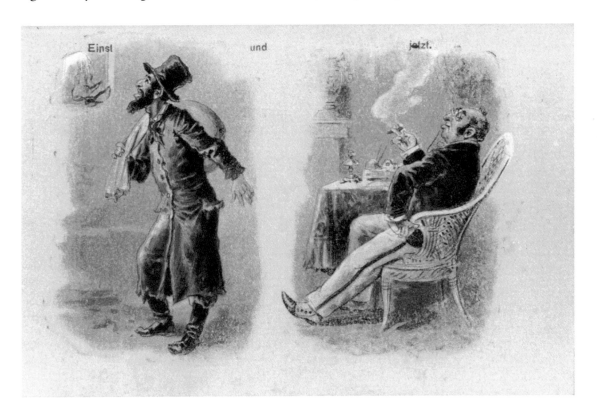

➤ *'The typical parasite, a sponger who like a noxious bacillus keeps spreading…'*

Mein Kampf, Volume 1, Adolf Hitler (1889-1945), published 1925, Munich

If Hitler was to become a credible leader of the nation, his undoubted ambition, then he needed a strong ideology and vision for the future. Whilst in prison after the 'Beer Hall Putsch' he wrote *Mein Kampf* ('My Struggle') a paranoid, crude, badly written book. In it he expressed his belief in the eternal struggle between the strong and the weak and, importantly, links strength and weakness to race. He describes 'the Jew' as *'the typical parasite, a sponger who like a noxious bacillus keeps spreading…'* and the urgent need for Aryans to conquer eastern Europe to secure their economic survival. One of Hitler's earliest followers, Emil Maurice, took down Hitler's dictation of the book in prison, and this volume is inscribed to Emil's mother.

1930-1934

THE IMPACT of the worldwide depression that followed the Wall Street Crash of 1929 was severe for Germany. By 1930 unemployment had reached up to four million, and the collapse of the large Danat-Bank in July 1931 worsened the economic situation and led to great hardship and unrest. Hitler exploited these problems for political gain, laying the blame for these crises on the Communists, the unfair punishment and persecution of the German people for the First World War, and the worldwide Jewish conspiracy. Without a clear political program of policies, the Nazis nevertheless grew in popularity, and in the elections of 1930, they won over 18 per cent of the vote, and became the second largest party in the Reichstag.

Hitler stood for election as President against the incumbent and war hero Paul von Hindenburg in early 1932. While he did not win, his campaign was brilliantly orchestrated by Joseph Goebbels, and his personal popularity grew. Hitler was flown around the country, arriving from the skies god-like, and Goebbels coordinated a nationwide campaign of propaganda that portrayed Hitler as a charismatic visionary, not just an ordinary politician. Subsequent elections to the Reichstag in July 1932 resulted in the Nazi party becoming the largest single parliamentary party. Further political crises later that year caused the government to lose a vote of no confidence. They opened negotiations with Hitler to form a new government together, and in January 1933 Hitler was appointed as Chancellor.

Under the guise of abolishing unemployment and poverty, Hitler began to systematically dismantle German civil liberties. In February 1933 the Reichstag was burned down by a Communist, which confirmed for many that Hitler's worldview was right. Hitler moved to consolidated his power and immediately began instituting such actions as boycotts against Jewish businesses, quotas on Jews in schools, and book burnings. Hindenburg died in August 1934 after which Adolf Hitler merged the offices of President, Chancellor and party leader into one. He had succeeded in becoming the dictator of Germany.

✑ 'Wir Wählen Hindenburg! Wir Wählen Hitler!',
election broadsheet, National Socialist German Workers' Party (NSDAP), 1932

This broadsheet was produced by the Nazi Party – the National Socialist German Workers' Party – probably for the presidential elections of March and April 1932. The headlines of it read; 'We vote Hindenburg! We vote Hitler! Look at these people and know where you belong!'. The portraits along the top half of the broadsheet depict politicians and public figures of the Weimar Republic. Some were Jewish, but not all of them. Some, like Albert Grzezinski and Adam Stegerwald, belonged to parties that were liberal or left wing, and therefore represented political opposition to the Nazis. Others were Marxists, such as Rudolf Hilferding, or socialists, like Arthur Crispien. Dr Johannes Bell, is singled out here because he was one of the two official German signatories of the Versailles peace treaty. (The other signatory, Hermann Müller, had died in 1931 which is presumably why he was not included here.) Dr Magnus Hirschfeld was a physician and sexologist whose advocacy for the rights of homosexuals and transgender people made him an obvious target of hate for the Nazis. Their portraits are headlined with the words 'We vote Hindenburg!' in a 'Jewish' style of typeface, made to look like Hebrew, and give the impression that they were all Jewish.

In contrast, the typeface used for the rest of the message, in which readers are exhorted to vote for Hitler, is one associated with the gothic, 'black letter', fonts favored by German nationalists. The men portrayed here as voting for Hitler were, of course, all members of the NSDAP by 1932. It is interesting to note that a number of them are shown wearing uniform, to emphasize the contrast with the civilians pictured above, and to establish the nationalist and military credentials of the Nazis. Three were recipients of one of the highest Prussian orders, Pour le Merité, during the war and Röhm had been awarded the Iron Cross First Class.

The 1932 presidential elections were a two-way contest between Paul von Hindenburg and Adolf Hitler. Hindenburg had been recalled from retirement upon the outbreak of war in 1914 and given command of the Eighth Army fighting on the eastern front. His early victories at Tannenburg and the Masurian Lakes against the Russians made him a national hero. Despite Germany's eventual defeat he retained this status and was elected President in 1925. By 1932 he was 84 years old and was persuaded to stand for re-election by his supporters who believed he was the only man who could beat Hitler. Hitler had moved away from the beer hall politics of the early 1920s, recognizing that such tactics were not gaining ground any longer. But by 1932 it was obvious that the short-lived governments of the Weimar Republic had failed to solve Germany's pressing economic and social problems. Hitler had focused his energies on transforming the image of the NSDAP into that of a parliamentary party, albeit one that made frequent, tactical, use of its paramilitary wing, the Stürmabteilung (SA – when translated – 'Assault Detachment'). The SA, commonly known as the 'Brownshirts' because of their uniforms, provided protection for the Nazi leadership, but also disrupted the meetings of opposing parties and engaged in violent street fighting and intimidation.

The fate of a number of the men portrayed in this broadsheet belies the true nature of Nazism. Of the ten 'Hindenburg voters', six fled or were forced into exile after Hitler became Chancellor in 1933. Of the Nazis, two were killed on Hitler's orders in July 1934 during the events now known as the 'Night of the Long Knives', when over 70 Nazi leaders and their followers were murdered, in a deliberate attempt to remove political rivals and eliminate the SA's power base.

Ticket for a National Socialist German Workers' Party (NSDAP) event, 6 October 1932, and poster advertising a Stürmabteilung (SA) rally, 30 October 1932

The Nazi Party had gained 18 per cent of the vote in the Reichstag elections of September 1930 to become the second largest political party. The economy continued to worsen with four million unemployed. Communists and Nazis caused mayhem and violence at each other's meetings and on the streets. These two documents from October 1932 illustrate the strength of the Nazis by this time – Hermann Göring was now President of the Reichstag; the Stürmabteilung (SA) was more than a quarter of a million men strong – more men than were in the German Army – and rallies like this one in Berlin made an impressive show of force.

SA.-Aufmarsch

Groß-Berlin
und
Brandenburg

am Sonntag, dem 30. Oktober 1932

Einlaß 12 Uhr

Anfang 1 Uhr

Gelände Schloß Schönholz
und im
Stadion Neukölln
Haupteingang Warthestraße

Einlaß 12 Uhr

Anfang 1 Uhr

Fahnenaufmarsch sämtlicher Sturmfahnen
Fliegerangriff des Fliegersturms Berlin-Brandenburg
Abwehr- und Gasschutzübungen der S.A.

Ansprachen:
Pgg. Dr. Goebbels, Graf Helldorff, Engel

Vorbeimarsch der gesamten S.A.-Formationen
Militärkonzert der gesamten S.A.-Musikkapellen

Eintritt 50 Pfg.
Den gesamten Erlös erhält die Winterhilfe der S.A. Berlin-Brandenburg (S.A.-Küchen)

Anmerkung: Auf beiden Plätzen wird das gleiche Programm vorgeführt. Der Kartenvertrieb erfolgt durch die S.A. und Vertriebsstellen des „Angriffs", sowie durch alle Zeugmeistereiläden.

Fahrverbindungen: Schloß Schönholz [Pankow-Reinickendorf Ost] Straßenbahnlinie 23, 45, 47, 51, 57, 88, 119, 199; Autobus 2 und 9; Vorortbahn Station Reinickendorf-Schönholz.

Stadion Neukölln Straßenbahn 27, 49; Untergrundbahn Station Leinestraße; Stadtbahn Bahnhof Hermannstraße.

This broadsheet, 'Down with Juda!', teems with violent, angry and aggressive words, and aimed at building on Hitler's unlikely success of becoming Chancellor of Germany in January 1933 and the subsequent declaration of the Third German Reich on 21 March. *'German soldier, you fought at the front. … the Jew grew fat behind the lines. … You, the German are the poor honest slave. The Jew is the treacherous and rich overlord. … Germans, march in step! ….. March with us in the struggle for the honor of your shining national revolution!'*

1000 Reichsmarks banknotes overprinted with Nazi antisemitic election slogans by the 'Völkischer Beobachter München' newspaper, 1932

These worthless banknotes from the period of hyperinflation of 1922-23 have been overprinted with Nazi election slogans, exhorting the reader to 'come to Hitler'. The fact that they are printed onto money – the symbol both of German vulnerability and of supposed Jewish economic domination – must have had particular resonance. The swastika sunrise was a recurring motif in the 1932 elections. The Nazi linkage between Jews and Communism is made clear through the image of Karl Radek. The description of him as; 'Train robber, murderer of workers' presumably references his involvement with the failed German Communist revolutions of 1919-20.

The appointment of Adolf Hitler as Chancellor in January 1933 had been rapidly followed by events that spurred many people, Jews included, to get out of the country. The burning down of the Reichstag (the parliament building) in February provided the excuse for the Nazis to launch greater persecution of their political opponents. Claiming that the arson attack was just the beginning of a Communist plot to overthrow the government, Hitler persuaded Hindenburg of the need to suspend civil liberties with an emergency decree. In March a concentration camp for people identified as political enemies of the Nazis was opened at Dachau and thousands of Communists were arrested and imprisoned without trial. Having eliminated their main parliamentary opposition, the Nazis were now able to put plans for the elimination of the Jews from Germany into action, and to do so through the apparatus of the state. Jews were dismissed from their jobs in the civil service and their shops were boycotted in April of that year. In May, mass book burnings were staged in several cities throughout Germany. Considerable pressure began to be applied to Jewish businessmen and tradespeople to sell up, at reduced rates. In addition to these initiatives, the Nazi regime turned its attention to existing laws and regulations to twist them in ways that could more specifically target Jews.

Nazi ideology held that the Jews were responsible for the economic ills of Germany, that they had stripped it of its wealth in the pursuit of their own personal greed and gain. The word 'Wiedergutmachung' was sometimes used to describe this idea, where its combined meanings of reparation, restitution and atonement illustrate the notion that Germans had suffered from this Jewish robbery, and therefore deserved the appropriate compensation. Nazi propaganda consistently portrayed Jews as being economically dominant. In reality, Jews accounted for just one per cent of the population of Germany. Regardless of this reality, much Nazi attention was paid to stripping Jews of their economic assets.

Pre-existing regulations had already restricted the export of German currency and stipulated that all emigrants had to pay twenty five per cent of their assets to the state in order to leave the country – in effect, a tax on emigration. This was increased in 1934 when the threshold at which taxation began was reduced in a deliberate decision to obtain more money from Jews wishing to emigrate. This five Reichsmark note was made and issued during the years 1933-1935 by the newly-created Conversion Office for German External Debts. The notes were issued to would-be emigrants on the basis that they could be exchanged for hard currency in other countries at their stated monetary value, in other words, at the value they had paid to the obtain the notes. This proved not to be the case. They were, in fact, mostly worthless, a fact only discovered by people after having left Germany for good. This particular note is in pristine condition, probably never used, a state that testifies to its worthlessness. The formalized system of taking money from Jewish emigrants generated much needed income for the Nazi regime and further, more aggressive, measures were implemented throughout the 1930s. The theft of Jewish assets to fund the German war effort is one of the least well-known aspects of Nazism.

'Der Stürmer'

'DER STÜRMER' ('The Storm'), published in Munich by Julius Streicher between 1923 and 1945, was the most vitriolic of all antisemitic newspapers in Germany. From small beginnings, the paper became so widely read that by 1935 its circulation was counted at more than 400,000 copies a week and newspaper cases featuring 'Der Stürmer' were also displayed in city centers throughout the Third Reich. The display cases were often paid for by loyal readers and adorned with slogans such as; 'The Jews are our misfortune' and; 'German women and girls, the Jews are your destruction'. Copies were distributed to centers of German émigré populations in the United States, Brazil and Canada amongst other countries.

The paper used basic vocabulary and short sentences, and after 1925, made liberal use of cartoons drawn by Philipp Rupprecht. Streicher became a well known figure throughout Germany and overseas.

He was accused and found guilty of being 'an accessory to the persecution of the Jews' by the International Military Tribunal in Nuremberg, and was hanged in 1946.

Der Stürmer' newspapers, 1935 and June 1939, Munich

'Der Stürmer' became the most infamous of Nazi newspapers. Run by Julius Streicher in Munich it survived on a diet of scandal stories and an unrelenting stream of antisemitic invective. The 1935 issue shown here declares; *Murderers since time immemorial. Jewish World Bolshevism from Moses to the Comintern .... Turmoil all over the world*', whilst that of June 1939 headlines with; *'The Talmud Court. The Victory of World Jewry'*. Streicher had been an elementary school teacher before the First World War, and used his publishing house to produce three antisemitic books aimed at young children.

38]

1935-1938

NAZI RESTRICTIONS on Jews had escalated from April 1933 onwards in a succession of measures that, for example, banned Jews from belonging to sports organisations, working as journalists on non-Jewish newspapers, taking law or medical exams, and belonging to the military. The so-called 'Nuremberg Laws' of September 1935 set out the most radical change of all. Overturning the past, the laws reconstituted Germany as a racial state, where citizenship was solely defined by a person's race. Jews were defined as a separate race, and were not eligible to participate in the life of the German state. A deluge of laws and restrictions followed

Jews lost the right to vote, they were excluded from or dismissed from the professions, forced to sell their businesses to German buyers at low prices, removed from universities and restricted from travelling overseas. Their further segregation from German society was implemented by banning them from using parks, restaurants, and swimming pools. 1938 saw a further spate of antisemitic measures, including the introduction of special identity cards for Jews, and the requirement that all Jewish men take the name 'Israel' as their middle name, and all women to take the name 'Sara'.

'Kristallnacht' (the 'Night of Broken Glass') occurred on the night of November 9 and 10, 1938. This violent pogrom, initiated by the Nazis, saw thousands of Jewish synagogues and business plundered and burned. Thousands of Jewish men were rounded up, jailed, and sent to concentration camps. Kristallnacht was the most violent turning point in the Nazi repression of the Jews.

Reichsbürgergesetz.

Vom 15. September 1935.

Der Reichstag hat einstimmig das folgende Gesetz beschlossen, das hiermit verkündet wird:

§ 1

(1) Staatsangehöriger ist, wer dem Schutzverband des Deutschen Reichs angehört und ihm dafür besonders verpflichtet ist.

(2) Die Staatsangehörigkeit wird nach den Vorschriften des Reichs- und Staatsangehörigkeitsgesetzes erworben.

§ 2

(1) Reichsbürger ist nur der Staatsangehörige deutschen oder artverwandten Blutes, der durch sein Verhalten beweist, daß er gewillt und geeignet ist, in Treue dem Deutschen Volk und Reich zu dienen.

(2) Das Reichsbürgerrecht wird durch Verleihung des Reichsbürgerbriefes erworben.

(3) Der Reichsbürger ist der alleinige Träger der vollen politischen Rechte nach Maßgabe der Gesetze.

§ 3

Der Reichsminister des Innern erläßt im Einvernehmen mit dem Stellvertreter des Führers die zur Durchführung und Ergänzung des Gesetzes erforderlichen Rechts- und Verwaltungsvorschriften.

Nürnberg, den 15. September 1935,
am Reichsparteitag der Freiheit.

Der Führer und Reichskanzler

Adolf Hitler

Der Reichsminister des Innern

Frick

Gesetz zum Schutze des deutschen Blutes und der deutschen Ehre.

Vom 15. September 1935.

Durchdrungen von der Erkenntnis, daß die Reinheit des deutschen Blutes die Voraussetzung für den Fortbestand des Deutschen Volkes ist, und beseelt von dem unbeugsamen Willen, die Deutsche Nation für alle Zukunft zu sichern, hat der Reichstag einstimmig das folgende Gesetz beschlossen, das hiermit verkündet wird:

§ 1

(1) Eheschließungen zwischen Juden und Staatsangehörigen deutschen oder artverwandten Blutes sind verboten. Trotzdem geschlossene Ehen sind nichtig, auch wenn sie zur Umgehung dieses Gesetzes im Ausland geschlossen sind.

(2) Die Nichtigkeitsklage kann nur der Staatsanwalt erheben.

§ 2

Außerehelicher Verkehr zwischen Juden und Staatsangehörigen deutschen oder artverwandten Blutes ist verboten.

§ 3

Juden dürfen weibliche Staatsangehörige deutschen oder artverwandten Blutes unter 45 Jahren in ihrem Haushalt nicht beschäftigen.

§ 4

(1) Juden ist das Hissen der Reichs- und Nationalflagge und das Zeigen der Reichsfarben verboten.

(2) Dagegen ist ihnen das Zeigen der jüdischen Farben gestattet. Die Ausübung dieser Befugnis steht unter staatlichem Schutz.

§ 5

(1) Wer dem Verbot des § 1 zuwiderhandelt, wird mit Zuchthaus bestraft.

(2) Der Mann, der dem Verbot des § 2 zuwiderhandelt, wird mit Gefängnis oder mit Zuchthaus bestraft.

(3) Wer den Bestimmungen der §§ 3 oder 4 zuwiderhandelt, wird mit Gefängnis bis zu einem Jahr und mit Geldstrafe oder mit einer dieser Strafen bestraft.

§ 6

Der Reichsminister des Innern erläßt im Einvernehmen mit dem Stellvertreter des Führers und dem Reichsminister der Justiz die zur Durchführung und Ergänzung des Gesetzes erforderlichen Rechts- und Verwaltungsvorschriften.

§ 7

Das Gesetz tritt am Tage nach der Verkündung, § 3 jedoch erst am 1. Januar 1936 in Kraft.

Nürnberg, den 15. September 1935,
am Reichsparteitag der Freiheit.

Der Führer und Reichskanzler

Adolf Hitler

Der Reichsminister des Innern

Frick

Der Reichsminister der Justiz

Dr. Gürtner

Der Stellvertreter des Führers

R. Heß
Reichsminister ohne Geschäftsbereich

Das Reichsgesetzblatt erscheint in zwei gesonderten Teilen — Teil I und Teil II —. Fortlaufender Bezug nur durch die Postanstalten. Bezugspreis vierteljährlich für Teil I = 1,75 ℛℳ, für Teil II = 2,10 ℛℳ. Einzelbezug jeder (auch jeder älteren) Nummer nur vom Reichsverlagsamt, Berlin NW 40, Scharnhorststraße Nr. 4 (Fernsprecher: D 2 Weidendamm 9265 — Postscheckkonto: Berlin 96700). Einzelnummern werden nach dem Umfang berechnet. Preis für den achtseitigen Bogen 15 ℛₚ, aus abgelaufenen Jahrgängen 10 ℛₚ, ausschließlich der Postbeischaffungsgebühr. Bei größeren Bestellungen 10 bis 60 v. H. Preisermäßigung.

Herausgegeben vom Reichsministerium des Innern. — Gedruckt in der Reichsdruckerei, Berlin.

The Nuremberg Laws, Reichsgesetzblatt (Reich Law Gazette), Volume 1, published 1935, Berlin

Once in power, the Nazi regime initiated hundreds of decrees and regulations aimed at limiting Jewish participation in civic life. Their first initiative was the Enabling Law that followed the Reichstag fire of 27 February 1933, which suspended many basic human rights – freedom of the press and of association – for all Germans. In April, Hitler assured President Hindenburg that a 'legal solution' to the 'Jewish problem' would follow. What was less clear, because it was so radical, was what Hitler and his party meant by this. Instead of building on existing legal precedent and practice, they overturned it. Beginning with Hitler's own views on humanity, the Nazi rejection of the ideas of the Enlightenment led to the conclusion that there was no equality between people. The racial and national inequalities between people meant that, in the Nazi worldview, there could be no equality in law. The first decrees of 1933 prevented Jews from working in the civil service, going to German schools or publishing their own newspapers. Following the unchallenged elimination of his political enemies during the 'Night of the Long Knives', Hindenburg's death and Hitler's merger of the Chancellorship with the Presidency in 1934, and a series of successes in foreign policy in 1935, Hitler decided he was strong enough to introduce further legislation.

The manner in which he did this reveals much about the nature of his leadership. NSDAP administrators had been drawing up proposals to place further restrictions on Jews for months, but Hitler had procrastinated. Then suddenly, on 13 September 1935, he instructed his Minister of the Interior, Wilhelm Frick, that he wanted to announce new legislation to regulate German-Jewish 'blood' relationships at the Party Rally, just two days later. Frick mobilized two of his best staff and flew a third in from Berlin overnight to work up a first draft. They proposed the Law for the Protection of German Blood and German Honor. Hitler accepted their first draft, and asked them for a second law that would define the status, rights and obligations of citizens. Again, he approved the first draft. Both laws were announced on 15 September.

The Reich Citizenship Law made a clear distinction between citizens, who could only be people 'of German or related blood', and subjects. Citizens enjoyed full rights and protection of the state. Subjects did not. And Jews were deemed to be subjects. The second law banned marriage or any sexual relations between Germans and Jews, punishable by imprisonment. The cornerstone of the racial state was now in place. What made a person a Jew was not clear at this point. Many of Germany's Jews were largely assimilated into German culture which meant that reaching a definition would be complicated. The distinctions made between people with one, two, three or four Jewish grandparents, or by the date at which ancestors had converted from Judaism to Christianity, seem ridiculous were it not for the fact that, within a few years of these laws being enacted, it came to mean life or death for people.

This image is of the relevant pages from the annual gazette of all laws published in 1935 for the German Reich; these two most revolutionary laws appear on pages 1146 and 1147. It perhaps seems extraordinary that they take up only two pages of the thousands produced in that year.

'Anyone who buys from a Jew is a traitor to his people'

('Wor beim Juden kauft ist ein Volksverräter') carved wooden plaque, date unknown, Nuremberg, and
'Ayran Shop' ('Arisches Geschäft'), enamel sign, date unknown

A nationwide boycott of Jewish shops and businesses was organized for Saturday 1 April 1933, just weeks after Hitler's appointment as German Chancellor. Groups of the Stürmabteilung (the SA) stood on the streets to intimidate and discourage people from shopping. Antisemitic slogans and the star of David were painted onto walls and windows. As the Nazi regime took hold, more permanent signs were made, such as this tin sign declaring shops to be 'Aryan' and 'German', or the more direct messaging of the carved wooden plaque from Nuremberg which translates as; 'Anyone who buys from a Jew is a traitor to his people'.

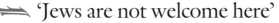 'Jews are not welcome here'
street signs from Berlin and Albertshof Bavaria

These signs declare Nazi allegiance by the presence of the swastika as well as through the words themselves. The wooden sign, 'Juden sind hier unerwünscht' ('Jews are not welcome here') comes from Berlin where the Gauleiter was Joseph Goebbels, Hitler's minister for propaganda in the 1930s. The double signs originate from a small town, Albertshof, in Bavaria, and have the added feature of declaring 'Unser Gruß ist "Heil Hitler!"', ('Our greeting is "Heil Hitler!"') Local Nazi parties began putting up signs like these from the spring of 1935 onwards, and following the Nuremberg Laws of September 1935, signs like these became even more common.

✐ Metal plaque banning Jews from using a park bench,

and leaflet discouraging Jews from visiting a spa resort in Bavaria

It was vital to the Nazi state that Jews become increasingly segregated. One of the most important aspects of Nazi anti-Semitism was an engendering of physical repulsion towards Jews, and in 1937-38, measures were encouraged to ensure that no physical contact whatsoever could take place between Jews and non-Jews. The black and white enameled sign bans Jews from sitting on a park bench. The small red paper slip announces that Jews are unwelcome in the spa resorts of Werdenfels in Bavaria. 250,000 of these slips were printed in February 1938 to be attached to tourism leaflets before their distribution within Germany.

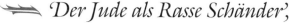 *'Der Jude als Rasse Schänder',*

Dr Kurt Plischke and Philipp Rupprecht, published 1934, Berlin

This book's title can be translated as 'The Jew as race desecrator', 'defiler', or 'abuser'. And the subtitle; 'An accusation of Judah and a reminder to German women and girls', leaves no room for doubt that the book expounds upon the purported sexual predator tendencies of all Jewish men towards non-Jewish women. The book comprises caricatures drawn by the regular cartoonist of 'Der Stürmer', Philip Rupprecht, that depict Jewish men as lascivious lechers bent on corrupting German women, and consequently, the racial purity of the German race. Rupprecht was sentenced to 6 years' hard labor in 1945 at the Nuremberg war crimes trial.

Information Office for Fostering Racial and Hereditary Matters leaflet, 'Werkblatt zur Ausfüllung der Sippentafel', Berlin

This leaflet was sent to Helga Fraenkel in response to her request for permission to marry an Aryan man, Gerhard Haupt, by the Information Office for Fostering Racial and Hereditary Matters of Schöneberg, Berlin. Following the Nuremberg Laws she had to provide detailed genealogical information about her parents and grandparents to prove her racial eligibility for the marriage. The leaflet gives detailed instructions for filling out the accompanying forms, including the everyday bureaucratic requirement that; *All statements must be made honestly and to the best of your knowledge*.

Defining Jewishness

Schriftenreihe des Reichsausfschusses für Volksgesundheitsdienst booklet (Series of the Reich Committee for Public Health Service), January 1937, Berlin

The definition of a Jew was developed by Nazi policy makers following the Nuremberg Laws. This table is from the booklet issued to Helga Fraenkel in response to her request for permission to marry an Aryan. It presents the pseudo-science of Nazi racial ideology, defining the extent of a person's 'Jewishness' by the religious affiliation of their grandparents. Those defined as 'full Jews' had three or four grandparents 'of the Jewish faith', whilst those with one or two such grandparents were branded a 'Mischling' – a 'half-breed'. The booklet shows passages underlined in pencil in Helga's attempts to make sense of them.

Helga Fraenkel's application to marry an Aryan

Helga Fraenkel made her first application for a marriage license to marry Gerhard Haupt in January 1938. She was 26 years old and already pregnant. Following the Nuremberg Laws of September 1935 it was necessary to establish her racial status before being given permission to marry Gerhard, who was a 'pure German'. Helga's papers show she had been born, baptized and confirmed as a Lutheran at the Gethsemane Church in Berlin. But Helga's father had been born to Jewish parents, Julius and Rosa. Having two grandparents of Jewish faith meant that Helga was categorized as a 'first degree Mischling', a half-breed. First degree Mischlinge were forbidden to marry Aryans or second degree Mischlinge to prevent the birth of further mixed race children.

If the Nazis claimed that their racial ideology was based on science, the reality is that it was simply invented so as to re-categorise Jews as being less than human – 'untermensch' – and to create the idea that their lives were worth less than those of 'pure' Germans. It was a necessary step to advance the exclusion of Jews from German society on 'rational' and 'legal' grounds. The slim file of papers that once belonged to Helga Fraenkel are a testament to the cruel consequences of Nazi ideology and the bureaucracy that translated it into policy. Beginning with her first application for a marriage license, Helga's papers trace her attempts to obtain the required certificates for her grandparents. In her letter to the Jewish Gemeinde of Berlin in March 1938, Helga expresses her optimism that the records will be easy to find since she thought that her great grandfather and his ancestors had been rabbis. Perhaps she was unaware that her status as a Mischling meant she was almost certainly going to be refused permission to marry Gerhard. Her hope, so naively expressed, was of course, hopeless. Whether the correct records could be found or not, there was no hiding the fact from Nazi authorities that she had two Jewish grandparents.

It was possible to attempt to be reclassified, by denying the paternity of the ancestor(s) in question. In other words, to declare that they were not the child of their named father, but of another – an illegitimate child. Despite the social shame and embarrassment of carrying out this procedure, cases soared following the Nuremberg Laws of 1935 and again in 1938-9 after the violence of Kristallnacht.

In May 1938 Helga gave birth to a boy, Jürgen Alfred Adolf.

Permission to marry his father Gerhard was refused on 25 February 1939. During the following year she filled out two forms with details of her own family relations, and for her son. These appear to be rough drafts for the final forms that she submitted to the authorities sometime after the birth of her second child, Gisela, in May 1939. The last document, dated 24 May 1941, informs Helga that her appeal against the refusal to grant her permission to marry has failed, and that any further attempts will be ignored and will be, therefore, 'futile'. It also informs her that the two photographs of her children have been returned to her. This is the last known trace of her.

The documents shown here are her rough draft of the genealogical questionnaire, and a photograph of her, noted on the back as having been taken in Lychen, Brandenburg, in 1935. Helga is indicated by the small cross drawn onto the photograph.

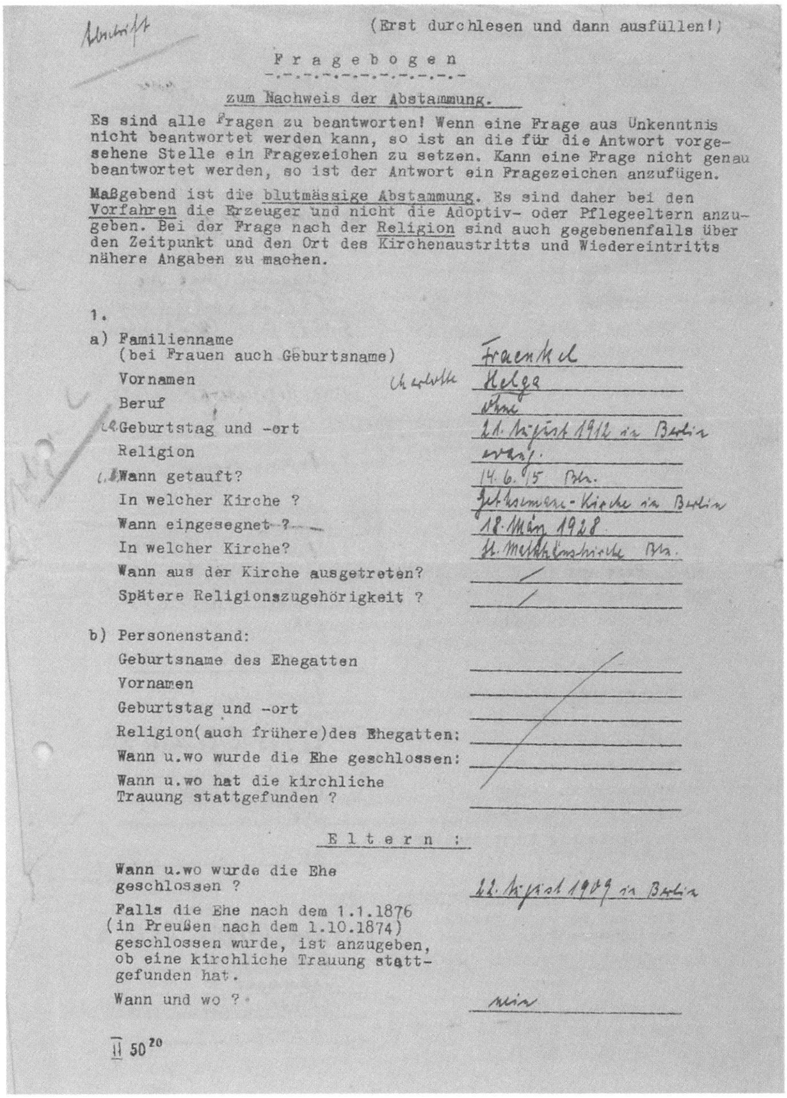

Abschrift (Erst durchlesen und dann ausfüllen!)

Fragebogen

zum Nachweis der Abstammung.

Es sind alle Fragen zu beantworten! Wenn eine Frage aus Unkenntnis nicht beantwortet werden kann, so ist an die für die Antwort vorgesehene Stelle ein Fragezeichen zu setzen. Kann eine Frage nicht genau beantwortet werden, so ist der Antwort ein Fragezeichen anzufügen.

Maßgebend ist die blutmässige Abstammung. Es sind daher bei den Vorfahren die Erzeuger und nicht die Adoptiv- oder Pflegeeltern anzugeben. Bei der Frage nach der Religion sind auch gegebenenfalls über den Zeitpunkt und den Ort des Kirchenaustritts und Wiedereintritts nähere Angaben zu machen.

1.

a) Familienname (bei Frauen auch Geburtsname) Fraenkel
Vornamen Charlotte Helga
Beruf ohne
Geburtstag und -ort 21. August 1912 in Berlin
Religion evang.
Wann getauft? 14.6.15 Bln.
In welcher Kirche ? Gethsemane-Kirche in Berlin
Wann eingesegnet ? 18. März 1928
In welcher Kirche? St. Matthäuskirche Bln.
Wann aus der Kirche ausgetreten? /
Spätere Religionszugehörigkeit ? /

b) Personenstand:
Geburtsname des Ehegatten
Vornamen
Geburtstag und -ort
Religion(auch frühere)des Ehegatten:
Wann u.wo wurde die Ehe geschlossen:
Wann u.wo hat die kirchliche Trauung stattgefunden ?

Eltern :

Wann u.wo wurde die Ehe geschlossen ? 22. August 1909 in Berlin
Falls die Ehe nach dem 1.1.1876 (in Preußen nach dem 1.10.1874) geschlossen wurde, ist anzugeben, ob eine kirchliche Trauung stattgefunden hat.
Wann und wo ? nein

II 50 20

➤ 'I affirm that I have no ties to, or relations with, Jews whatsoever.'
Alfred Rosenberg's (1893-1946) declaration of loyalty, 9 July 1932

Alfred Rosenberg was very influential on Hitler's thinking, especially in cementing the link between 'world Jewry' and Bolshevism. Born in the Baltic region of the Russian Empire, Rosenberg's early life was profoundly shaped by the First World War and the Bolshevik revolution. Rivalry between leading Nazis for Hitler's favor was intense, and doubts raised over Rosenberg's racial status led to this declaration of July 1932. Point 1 reads; *'I affirm that I have no ties to, or relations with, Jews whatsoever.'* As easily as that, Rosenberg dismissed the problem and retained his role in the Nazi Party. He was found guilty of war crimes and hanged at Nuremberg in October 1946.

'Das Schwarze Korps' newspaper was the official paper for the Schutzstaffel (SS), the Nazi's paramilitary organization. Its name references the dominant color – black – for the prewar SS uniform, whilst the use of red on this front page references the choice of that color for the Nazi Party – and eventually the national German – flag. Beneath the typically Germanic type of the title favored by the Nazis as representative of 'true' Germanic, Nordic culture, the letters 'SS' are rendered in the runic alphabet. The use of symbols like these served to build up a cultish sense of a mystical, meaningful, political movement.

‏‎🪶‎ Hermann Göring's bookplate

This is the personal bookplate of Hermann Göring, found inside a luxuriously leather-bound copy of 'World Anti-Semitism in Words and Pictures'. This copy was published in 1936 in Dresden. Its subtitle, 'The world dispute over the Jewish Question' and its dedication to the violently antisemitic Julius Streicher for his, 'tireless and dedicated struggle against the Jews', reveals it to be propaganda rather than the scholarly work that its authorship by a variety of professors might otherwise indicate. The book makes use of illustrations, photographs and text quoting the work and words of others to depict a history of anti-Semitism, from Egyptian and Roman times through to the twentieth century. It describes the attitude and actions towards Jews of the medieval Popes and the Catholic church, the crusaders, Martin Luther, and Christopher Columbus amongst others. The authors describe anti-Semitism in France, Russia, Austria-Hungary and Germany, and many of the illustrations are used as evidence of the claim that Jews were determined to destroy European, and especially German, culture of the modern era. They compare images of Jews, their deviant art and debauchery, with those of the Nordic ideal. The fact that there is a long history to anti-Semitism is one of the most uncomfortable and difficult issues to address. It gave the Nazis the material they needed to position their own brand of anti-Semitism in an historical context and thereby construct a credible foundation for it. Once established as an ideology with plausible roots, the Nazis encouraged its radicalization, leading this effort through its own policies, propaganda and activity, but also enabling its propagation by others.

Just as important was the establishment of the Nazi ideal. Identification of an enemy 'other' can only truly succeed where there is an ideal culture against which it can be unfavorably compared. Göring's bookplate provides some fascinating insights into this Nazi ideal. The central figure is the Christian martyr and soldier saint, George, slaying the dragon from his pure white horse. St George is one of the most celebrated patron saints. His connection with the Teutonic Knights, a medieval order of soldier priests that had eventually come to settle in central Europe, made him a compelling symbol for the Nazis. Both Hitler and Heinrich Himmler were fascinated by medieval history and mysticism and Himmler used the Teutonic colors of black, symbolizing constancy, prudence and wisdom, and white, symbolizing truth, purity and sincerity, for the prewar uniforms for the SS (Schutzstaffel).

The words 'Ehre' (Honor), 'Freiheit' (Freedom), 'Wahrheit' (Truth) and 'Brot' (Bread) explain the vital linkage between these knightly, honorable, German values and the absolute need to provide bread (food) to sustain them. The idea of conquering other peoples and lands to provide one's own people with the basic means of survival is nothing new. But the Nazis, following Hitler's lead, believed that Jews were the main obstacle to attaining the resources needed to sustain and grow a Greater Germany and to enrich its Volk (people). The smaller image of the knight's armored arm holding a ring is Göring's personal seal, where the arm represents a person in a senior leadership position, and the ring represents fidelity. Göring first met Hitler in October 1922. He was thirty years old, a decorated hero of the First World War and became one of Hitler's earliest, most devoted, followers. He would become one of the key architects of the persecution and genocide of Europe's Jews during the war. Göring's love of hunting, the arts, military culture and regalia can all be discerned in this bookplate design. By 1936, however, he embodied little of the Nazi ideal himself, having grown obese and dependent on painkillers.

Antisemitic imagery in everyday objects

All three of these objects were made to engender disdain. The ashtrays offer two stereotypes of Jews: the itinerant peddler with his long beard and tray of goods, although this one is empty except for the word 'Jüdische' and looks more like a begging tray; and the exaggerated features of a grimacing Jew of the ceramic ashtray. The act of flicking ash and stubbing out cigarettes in ashtrays like these must have felt very satisfying to the owners. Similarly, the tight grip required on the elongated nose of the carved walking stick handle, tight enough to block all breathing, must have aroused powerful feelings of contempt.

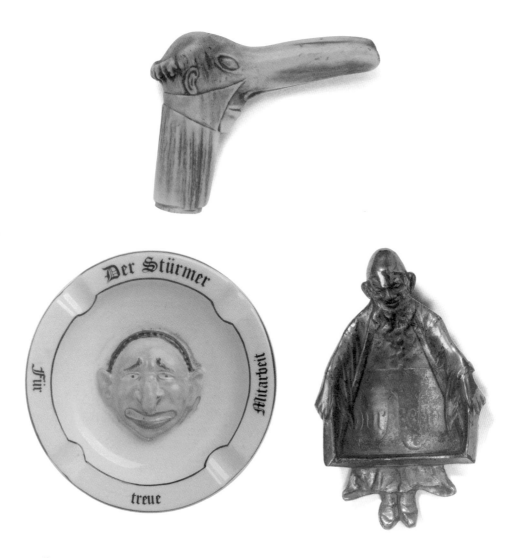

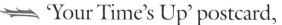 ‘Your Time's Up’ postcard,
published at the time of the annexation of Austria to the German Reich, 1938

German troops marched into Austria on 12 March 1938. The country was annexed to the German Reich. Looting of businesses, violence and public humiliation for Vienna's Jewish population quickly followed. Adolf Eichmann was put in charge of 'solving the Jewish problem' and his methods of persecution and deportation became the model for subsequently Nazi-occupied countries during the war. The illustration on this postcard caricatures the expulsion of Austrians and Jews by the Nazis; the red and white colors of the Austrian flag are shown on the boy and running man; the Jew at the back can be seen clutching his cashbox to his chest. The slogan reads; 'Your time's up!'.

Nazi Propaganda Literature and Art Exhibitions, 1937-1938

DURING THE 1930S the Nazi propaganda machine had become very efficient in reaching the German people not only through mass rallies and newspapers, but through literature and art exhibitions as well. Children's books ensured that indoctrination into Nazi antisemitic ideology began at a very early age. Art exhibitions were staged to expose, in the words of Adolf Ziegler, who spoke at the opening of the 'Entartete Kunst' ('Degenerate Art') exhibition, a; '. . . monstrous offspring of insanity, impudence, ineptitude, and sheer degeneracy'. His attacks also insinuated that Jewish art dealers were behind this undermining of a 'pure' German culture. Other exhibitions, such as 'Der Ewige Jude' ('The Eternal Jew') constituted more direct attacks on Jews.

Das ist der Jud, das sieht man gleich
der größte Schuft im ganzen Reich!
Er meint, daß er der Schönste sei
Und ist so häßlich doch dabei!

Der Deutsche ist
ein stolzer Mann
der arbeiten
und kämpfen kann.
Weil er so schön ist
und voll Mut,
haßt ihn von jeher
schon der Jud!

'…the German stands up, the Jew gives way.'

'Trust No Fox' children's book, published 1936, Munich

This book is one of three published for children by the 'Der Stürmer' publishing house in 1936. Literally translated the title reads; 'Trust no fox on his green heath and no Jew on his oath', which is a phrase taken from the sixteenth century German Protestant theologian and reformer, Martin Luther. A total of 100,000 copies were printed and distributed to schools, free of charge. The book was written by Elvira Bauer, an eighteen year old kindergarten teacher, and promulgates antisemitic views by contrasting the qualities of Germans and Jews. It is written as a series of rhymes that are colorfully illustrated. Bauer described Germans as being tall, blond, handsome, racially pure and therefore healthy. They work hard and honestly. In contrast, she portrayed Jews as the opposite; short, dark, with exaggerated and disfigured facial features. They appear shifty, threatening, as parasites who live off the hard work of others. The book acts as a primer for children in guiding them through some of the fundamental aspects of Nazi anti-Semitism. It reiterates a medieval idea that the Jews were disciples of the devil; that they were condemned to a life of rootlessness following their betrayal of Jesus and his subsequent crucifixion; and that they were a malevolent presence in German society that should be expelled.

The page shown here make the contrast between Germans and Jews very clear. The blond German farm worker stands tall, his strong frame has been drawn in a few, simple, lines and block colors. The Jew has been drawn as short, fat, dark – physically repulsive. His briefcase, cigar, newspaper and pencil indicate an urban life of living off the toil of others rather than the honest work of himself. Child readers are exhorted to; *'Take a good look at the two in the picture drawn for you … Easy to guess which is which, I say: the German stands up, the Jew gives way.'*

During the war crimes trials at Nuremberg, this book, and another picture book 'The Poisonous Mushroom' were introduced as evidence during the testimony of Julius Streicher. He was one of Hitler's earliest followers and had published the virulently antisemitic newspaper 'Der Stürmer' from 1923 to the end of the war in 1945. Streicher reveled in his reputation as the chief 'Jew-baiter' of the Nazi regime, and his conduct became so extreme that he was stripped of his official duties in 1940. Yet he and Hitler remained on good personal terms, and he was allowed to continue to publish. Questioning of Streicher was cut short when he persisted in making repeated references to a pre-war trial of an alleged child molester, who was Jewish, and whose trial he claimed had provided the motivation for writing and publishing these two books. No doubt he wished to regale the courtroom with details of the alleged offences and thereby provide more of the sort of lurid, pornographic, content that he was infamous for publishing. One of most important elements of all the antisemitic education of children was to enforce the idea of racial purity of the German race, and to indoctrinate children to avoid any interaction with Jews whatsoever, so that the grave risk of genetic contamination could be eliminated. Streicher was found guilty and hanged as a war criminal for inciting racial hatred, murder and extermination, at Nuremberg in October 1946.

~~~ *'Der Giftpilz' ('The Poisonous Mushroom')*

children's book, published 1938, Munich, and 'Juden stellen sich vor' ('Jews Introduce Themselves'), book, published 1934, Munich

'Der Giftpilz' ('The Poisonous Mushroom') is a children's story book, published in 1938 by Julius Streicher's publishing house. The brightly illustrated stories strive to inculcate its young readers with the falsehoods and stereotypes about Jews that the Nazi regime needed to sustain. Children were warned that, like mushrooms, some Jews could seem benign but were in fact poisonous. 'Juden stellen sich vor' ('Jews Introduce Themselves'), published in 1934, consists of full-page black and white caricatures of Jews – the peddler, the boss, and the butcher, amongst others. There is some suggestion that this was intended to be a coloring book for children.

As a young man, Hitler had hoped to study at the Vienna Academy of Art and become a great artist. But his application for admission was rejected, twice. His drawings and paintings show only a moderate level of skill and are conventional in content and execution. For Hitler, modernism had unpleasant and dangerous connections with Jews and their supposed ambition to dominate every aspect of culture, to the detriment of 'true' German culture. Once in power, the Nazi Party was able to begin to expunge all traces of this 'degenerate' art from the country's art galleries, museums and collections. The offending art was defined as being works that; *'insult German feeling, or destroy or confuse natural form or simply reveal an absence of adequate manual and artistic skill'*. The most infamous example of this policy is perhaps the exhibition of 'degenerate art' that opened in Munich in July 1937. Over 650 paintings, sculptures, prints and books that had been confiscated from museums in Germany were put on display. They were deliberately exhibited in a chaotic way, with derogatory text about the works daubed onto the walls, such as 'madness becomes method', 'nature as seen by sick minds', and 'even museum bigwigs called this the "art of the German people"'. Information about the price that museums had paid to originally buy the works was also included, to emphasize how German taxpayers had been 'fleeced' by Jewish artists and their dealers.

The exhibition was mounted to educate Germans about the sort of art that was unacceptable in Nazi society, to tutor them to despise it. Following its successful run in Munich, the exhibition travelled to other venues until 1941, by which time it had been seen by almost 3 million people. In contrast, the exhibition of 'Great German Art' had opened in Munich at the same time in 1937, intended to instruct Germans as to the qualities of culturally pure and German art. This was not nearly so well attended.

The work of some important artists was exhibited in the degenerate art show, including that of Marc Chagall, Max Ernst, Georg Grosz, Ernst Ludwig Kirchner, Wassily Kandinsky, Paul Klee and Emil Nolde. Nolde had been an enthusiastic supporter of the Nazis in the 1920s, and claimed that Expressionism was a distinctively Germanic art movement, but his work was nevertheless later branded as degenerate. Many of the works that had been exhibited in the exhibition were later sold off to foreign buyers and museums in order to raise money for the German government.

The cover of this original catalogue for the exhibition features a sculpture by Otto Freundlich, 'Der Neue Mensch' ('The New Man'). Freundlich was a German Jewish artist, one of the first abstract artists who had organized the first Dada exhibition in 1919. By the mid-1920s he had moved to live and work in France. He was murdered at Majdanek concentration camp on the day he arrived in 1943. 'Der Neue Mensch' has never been recovered and is assumed to have been destroyed.

Of the 112 artists whose works were exhibited as 'degenerate', only six were Jewish.

'The Eternal Jew' ('Der Ewige Jude') exhibition catalogue, 1937 and souvenir postcard published by 'Der Morgen' newspaper

A further exhibition, 'Der Ewige Jude' ('The Eternal Jew') was opened at the end of 1937 to exhibit the 'outward characteristics' of Jews; in reality, an exhibition of antisemitic material. The front cover of the exhibition catalogue comprises a caricature of a 'wandering' Jew, dressed in Middle Eastern clothing, holding bloodstained coins and a whip in his hands, and Russia under his arm, all denoting his supposed control of the world through financial institutions and Bolshevism. The postcard was designed to be sent as a souvenir of the exhibition by 'Der Morgen' newspaper. This one was posted from Vienna in September 1938.

1939

THE SITUATION in Germany and Austria deteriorated and for many Jews, made it clear that they had to leave in order to survive Hitler's dire intentions. At the beginning of the year, Hitler warned of the possible 'annihilation of the Jewish race in Europe' should a second world war break out. The tone of this speech was his most threatening yet. Jews desperately tried get passports and the necessary paperwork that would allow them to emigrate. Some Jews were successful, as evidenced by the Gundelfinger family's flight from Würzburg, Germany, through the Netherlands to freedom in England, in August 1939.

What, in the 1920s, had first been just a single line in small lettering – almost a footnote – 'Jews not welcomed', at the bottom of broadsides announcing rallies, was now the law of the land. Few had taken Hitler very seriously in 1920 and even fewer would have been able to conceive of the evil that would consume the Nazis and Germany just fifteen years later.

⟨ Paying for Kristallnacht
Jewish Capital Levy notice, 21 January 1939

On 21 November 1938 the 'Decree Concerning the Atonement Fee for the Jews of German Citizenship' was issued. It required all Jews to pay 20% of their registered assets to the state. This letter was sent to Moriz Rosenfeld, a bookkeeper living in Vienna, informing him about the new tax and how to pay it. (Since the Anschluss of March 1938 Austria was considered to be part of the German Reich.) The decree was a direct consequence of the events of 9/10 November 1938, known subsequently as 'Kristallnacht', when Jewish people, homes, synagogues and businesses were subjected to violent attack. The name Kristallnacht references the large amount of broken glass that littered the streets following the pogrom. The violence was initially encouraged and organized by Nazi Party officials and members of the Stürmabteilung (SA) and Hitler Youth as part of the deliberate escalation and radicalization of action against the Jewish population. 91 Jews were killed. 30,000 Jewish men were arrested and imprisoned in concentration camps. Approximately 7,500 Jewish shops and businesses were attacked and vandalized, and over 260 synagogues were destroyed throughout Germany, Austria and the Sudetenland. The violence continued in the following days, with rises in rape and suicide rates noted in official police records.

The Decree was established to make the Jews pay the costs of repair for the damage done by the rioters on Kristallnacht by way of 'atonement' – 'Sühne'. Jews were instructed to make the payment in four instalments, due on 15 December 1938 and on 15 February, May and August 1939. This proforma letter advises recipients to pay by check rather than cash in order to avoid long queues for the cashier at the tax office. It also advises that late payments will incur an additional charge of 2% of the remaining debt. The thoroughness with which this new tax was implemented is evidenced by the fact that this letter was sent to Rosenfeld to inform him that he owed 0 (zero) Reichsmarks. In all, the tax raised one billion Reichsmarks. The theft of Jewish assets turned out to be far more successful and efficient when approached as an administrative task. Having subverted the laws of the state, the Nazi regime was able to steal money and property simply by introducing a new tax and using government departments to administer its implementation.

Nevertheless, the overt and physical violence of Kristallnacht was a significant turning point in the persecution of the Jews. The largely apathetic response of the German population signaled that they would tolerate more radical policies yet. Dozens of new laws and decrees were enacted over the following weeks to further strip Jews of civic and legal rights and exclude them from German society. Any remaining Jewish children in German schools were expelled; Jews were forbidden from owning cars or going to 'German' theatres, cinemas and concert halls, and their ability to use public transport was restricted. Hermann Göring called a meeting just days after Kristallnacht to plan more aggressive measures for removing Jews from the economy.

Jews were forbidden to continue running their businesses and were forced to sell their assets and property at prices far below market value. All purchases and subsequent sales to Aryan buyers were made through government-appointed representatives, and considerable profits were made for the Reich. Eventually all Jewish property came to be owned by the German state. The implementation of such radical measures persuaded many that it was time to leave Germany, and emigration rates soared as a result.

Identity card ('Kennkarte') belonging to Max Reinhold, 1939

From July 1938 all people living in Germany were required to apply for an identity card authorized by the police. They were usually made from a tear-resistant form of linen cloth so that they would be durable. To obtain a card people had to produce proof of their identity and be fingerprinted. 'Kennkarten' for Jews were marked with a large letter 'J' on the front and inside, as can be seen in this ID card for Max Reinhold. This was issued on 9 March 1939 in Dresden. From 1 January that year, all Jews had been required to add either 'Israel' or 'Sara' to their names, as another way of clearly identifying them.

Escaping persecution

Passports issued to Peppi Stern, Siegfried and Stefanie Gundelfinger, July 1939

The rise in violence towards Jews in Germany and Austria led to a surge in the number of people attempting to emigrate during 1938 and 1939. President Franklin Roosevelt called an international conference in response to mounting political pressure to address the problem of the increased numbers of refugees. Delegates from 32 countries met at Evian in July 1938 to express sympathy, but only one state, the Dominican Republic, agreed to take in more refugees. Immigration to the USA was so difficult that the annual quota for Germany was unfilled for this same year. Hopeful immigrants had to provide evidence of two sponsors who were already resident or citizens of the USA, multiple copies of bank statements, tax returns, affidavits of good conduct from the German Police authorities as well as the usual evidence in support of their identity.

For people like the Gundelfingers, applying for a visa to leave their homeland must have been difficult on a purely administrative level, even without the emotional and economic upheaval that

Unterschrift des Paßinhabers

Siegfried Franz Gundelfinger

und seiner Ehefrau

Es wird hiermit bescheinigt, daß der Inhaber die durch das obenstehende Lichtbild dargestellte Person ist und die darunter befindliche Unterschrift eigenhändig vollzogen hat.

........................., den ....

Beruf *Privatier*
Geburtsort *Michelbach*
Geburtstag *7.9.1881*
Wohnort *Würzburg*
Gestalt *mittel*
Gesicht *oval*
Farbe der Augen *braun*
Farbe des Haares *grau*
Besond. Kennzeichen *ohne*

Ehefrau

KINDER

Name	Alter	Geschlecht

2   3

it would entail. The three passports shown here tell the story of their emigration from their home in Würzburg. Siegfried and Stefanie had both been born in nearby Michelbach bei Gerabronn. They married in 1919 when Siegfried was 38 and Stefanie was 26. In January the following year, their daughter Emma Marianna was born. Siegfried's profession is recorded as being a wine merchant. By 1939, Stefanie's mother Peppi Stern was perhaps living with them in Würzburg. From the various reference numbers on their emigration paperwork, they certainly seem to have made their applications together. All three of their passports bear the large red letter 'J' and the addition of the names 'Israel' for Siegfried and 'Sara' for Peppi and Stefanie, in compliance with the requirements of the German state. They also show that each one of them was able to take only ten Reichsmarks in currency with them when they left.

The pages of their passports show that Siegfried, Stefanie and her mother Peppi travelled together from Germany, via the Netherlands to Britain, arriving at Harwich on the east coast, on 11 August 1939. By the end of that month, they had arrived in Derbyshire and registered as 'aliens' with the Police there. The British government did not apply quotas to immigration, and in fact much of its policy was discretionary. But Jews were taken in only on a temporary basis on the assumption that they would move on to other countries. The Gundelfingers were

74]

PERSONENBESCHREIBUNG		Ehefrau
Beruf *ohne*		
Geburtsort *Michelbach*		
Geburtstag *10.8.1893*		
Wohnort		
Gestalt *mittel*		
Gesicht *oval*		
Farbe der Augen *blau-grau*		
Farbe des Haares *blond*		
Besond. Kennzeichen *ohne*		

Unterschrift des Paßinhabers

Stefanie Sara Gundelfinger.

und seiner Ehefrau

Es wird hiermit bescheinigt, daß der Inhaber die durch das obenstehende Lichtbild dargestellte Person ist und die darunter befindliche Unterschrift eigenhändig vollzogen hat.

................., den................

KINDER		
Name	Alter	Geschlecht

no exception to this rule, since their visa stamp was accompanied by the statement that entry had been granted, *'on condition that the holder will emigrate from the UK and will not take any employment or engage in any business, profession or occupation in the UK.'* However, a death notice for Peppi Stern was published on 30 March 1945 and reveals that she had died in February – in Derbyshire – after 'suffering greatly'. A year later, the 'London Gazette' lists Siegfried as having been granted British citizenship – together with his daughter Emma. These small traces of an entire family provide a mere glimpse of the consequences of the Nazi racial state for individuals whose lives were permanently and cruelly disrupted by it.

It is difficult not to apply hindsight when considering the Gundelfingers' flight from Germany, but it is a fact that this small family entered Britain just a matter of weeks before war in Europe broke out and all visas were cancelled.

~ *'… if the international Jewish financiers in and outside Europe should succeed in plunging the nations once more into a world war, then the result will not be the Bolshevization of the earth, and thus the victory of Jewry, but the annihilation of the Jewish race in Europe!'*

Adolf Hitler's (1889-1945) handwritten notes for his speech of 30 January 1939

From 1933 onwards, Hitler usually made a speech on 30 January to mark the anniversary of his coming to power as Chancellor. His speech of 30 January 1939 is noted now for its use of the word 'annihilation' in relation to Nazi plans for resolving the 'Jewish Question'. But at the time, the harsher, more extreme language he had used was barely noted in the press and public reaction. Hitler spoke for two and a half hours, and covered many familiar subjects about which his statements were largely repetitious of previous ones. He had already been speaking for two hours by the time he reached the subject of Jewish emigration from Germany.

Erster Erfolg: 3,
Nicht Fortbestand - gebaut
Vermögen
        sondern Genie
        entspricht.
        Ich selbst
Vom Bauarbeiter.

2.) Neue Wirtschafts
        politik.
    Unser Kapital.
1913 — 1918 — 1933.
        Nur um?
Arbeit = unser Kapital

Unsere neue Führung! 4
Nat. soz. Wirtschaft
        politik.

3.) Neue Außenpolitik
    Nicht Genf.
            Moskau —
        sondern
        Deutschland
        Kraft. Stärke
    Wehrmacht.
            Folge: 1938

The speech was made at a time when negotiations between Germany and the representative for the Intergovernmental Committee on Refugees established by the Evian conference of July 1938, American lawyer George Rublee, had been underway for some months. The negotiations were foundering on Germany's refusal to allow Jewish property or assets to be used to pay for the costs of emigrating Jews. A plan had been proposed by which Jewish communities would finance the costs for 150,000 Jews to leave Germany over a three year period at a cost of one and a half billion Reichsmarks. But this was obviously a bitter bargain to have to strike with Germany, and negotiations were slow and difficult. This is what Hitler referenced in his speech when he declared; *In connection with the Jewish question I have this to say; it is a shameful spectacle to see how the whole democratic world is oozing sympathy for the poor tormented Jewish people, but remains hard-hearted and obdurate when it comes to helping them which is surely, in view of its attitude, an obvious duty.*

The most quoted part of this statement is as follows; *In the course of my life I have very often been a prophet, and have usually been ridiculed for it. During my struggle for power it was mostly the Jewish race that received my prophecies with laughter when I said that I would one day take over the leadership of the state, and with it that of the whole nation ('Volk'), and that I would then among many*

78]

other things bring the Jewish problem to a solution. Their laughter was uproarious, but I think that for some time now they have been laughing on the other side of their face.

Today I will once more be a prophet: if the international Jewish financiers in and outside Europe should succeed in plunging the nations once more into a world war, then the result will not be the Bolshevization of the earth, and thus the victory of Jewry, but the annihilation of the Jewish race in Europe!'

These six handwritten pages are Hitler's own notes for his speech. The word 'Judenfragen' ('Jewish questions') is penciled in red on the second page.

The speech was not the first time that Hitler or the Nazi leadership had used the word 'Vernichtung' (annihilation) when referring to Jews but its coupling of these plans with the threat of a new world war signaled a change in emphasis. The threat against the Jews was now being expressed within a more violent context. A new war on a global scale was rightly feared by all rational leaders and the peoples they governed, but not Hitler. And whilst there were many more decisions to be taken before the events that are known today as the Holocaust could take place, Hitler's fanatical anti-Semitism was as central to his dystopian vision of the perfect future in 1939 as it had been twenty years earlier.

KENNETH W. RENDELL is the Founder and Executive Director of the Museum of World War II, Boston. The Museum houses the most comprehensive collection of original artifacts and documents anywhere in the world. The exhibits and archives uniquely tell the human story interwoven with the social, economic, political and military events throughout the world, on home fronts and battlefronts. He began the collection in 1959 and pursued this interest when no other private or public collections were being formed. He opened the present building as a private museum in 2000 and opened to the public as a non-profit in 2013.

He is the author of *With Weapons and Wits, Psychological Warfare in World War II* (1990), *World War II, Saving the Reality* (2009), and *Politics, War and Personality, Fifty Iconic World War II Documents That Changed the World* (2013).

In his career as the leading dealer in historical documents he authored the basic reference works, *Forging History, the Detection of Fake Documents and History Comes to Life.*

SAMANTHA HEYWOOD is Museum Director and Director of Exhibitions at the Museum of World War II Boston. During her twenty-year career at Imperial War Museums she worked across major education and exhibition projects, culminating as Director of Public Programmes, and with the re-opening of IWM London's new atrium and First World War Galleries in 2014.

She is the author of *Churchill (Questions and Analysis in History)* (2003) and edited *Making Their Past Your Future* (2011) and the book of *The World War 1 Centenary Exhibition* (2015).

Typeset in Galliard and Wihelmklingsporschrift.
Design and typography by Jerry Kelly.